REVISED AND UPDATED

Transportation Around the World

Motorbikes

Chris Oxlade

Heinemann Library
Chicago, Illinois

©2001, 2008 Heinemann Library
a division of Reed Elsevier Inc.
Chicago, Illinois

Customer Service 888-454-2279
Visit our website at www.heinemannraintree.com

Designed by Kimberly R. Miracle, Ray Hendren, Cavedweller Studio and Q2A Creative
Printed in China by South China Printing Company

12 11 10 09 08
10 9 8 7 6 5 4 3 2 1

New edition ISBN-10:   1-4329-0202-4 (hardcover)
                         1-4329-0211-3 (paperback)
New edition ISBN-13:   978-1-4329-0202-5 (hardcover)
                         978-1-4329-0211-7 (paperback)

The Library of Congress has cataloged the first edition as follows:
Oxlade, Chris.
          Motorbikes / Chris Oxlade.
                    p. cm. — (Transportation around the world)
          Includes bibliographical references (p.   ) and index.
ISBN 1-57572-305-0 (library binding)
1.   Mopeds — Juvenile literature. [1. Mopeds.] I. Title. II. Series.

TL443 .095 2001
629.227'5 — dc21

                                                                    00-010064

Acknowledgments
The publisher would like to thank the following for permission to reproduce photographs: R.D. Battersby pp. **4**, **6**, **15**, **17**, **23**; Corbis pp. **12** (Reuters), **27** (Zefa/Jon Feingersh); Eye Ubiquitous p. **20**; Getty Images p. **13** (The Image Bank/Moritz Steiger); PA Photos p. **29**; PhotoEdit p. **24** (Dennis MacDonald); Pictures p. **25**; Quadrant pp. **9**, **11**, **14**, **18**, **21**, **22**, **26**; Science and Society Picture Library p. **8**; Tony Stone Images p. **19**; Travel Ink p. **28** (Tim Lynch); TRH Pictures pp. **5** (Gilera), **7**, **10**, **16**.

Cover photograph of a motocross rider reproduced with permission of Getty Images (Jim Arbogast).

Contents

Some words are shown in bold, **like this**. You can find out what
they mean by looking in the glossary.

What Is a Motorbike?

A motorbike is a machine with an **engine** that moves along on two or three wheels. There is a seat for a rider, and sometimes for a passenger. People call some motorbikes "motorcycles," or just "bikes."

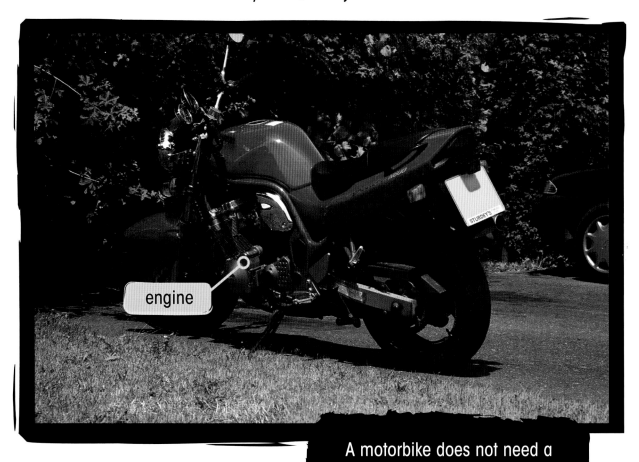

engine

A motorbike does not need a lot of space to park.

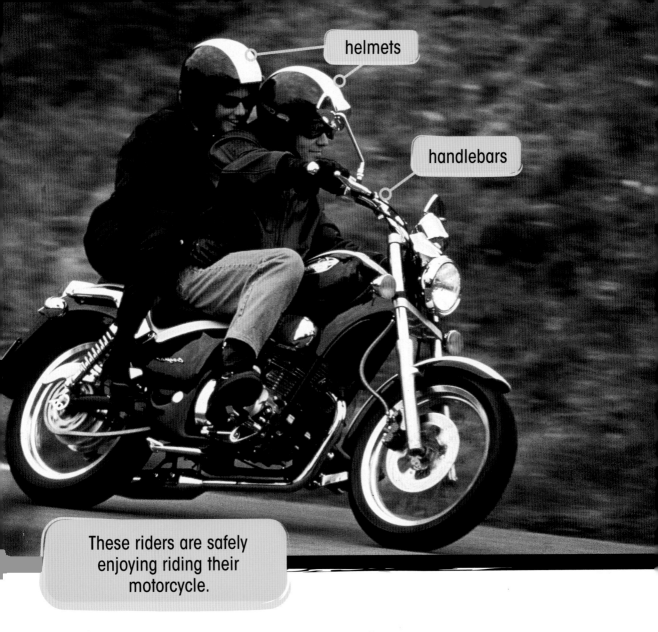

helmets

handlebars

These riders are safely enjoying riding their motorcycle.

The rider steers a motorbike to the left or right using the handlebars. Controls on the handlebars make the motorbike go faster or slower. The rider should always wear a helmet for safety.

How Motorbikes Work

Most motorbikes have two wheels. Each wheel has a **rubber tire** around it. The tires grip the road and stop the motorbike from sliding sideways as it goes around corners.

The wide tires on this motorcycle help make it safe to ride.

tire

This is the rear wheel
of a motorcycle.

A motorbike has an **engine** that makes the rear wheel turn. It is connected to the wheel with a chain. The engine needs **fuel** to make it work.

Old Motorbikes

This strange machine was one of the first motorbikes.

One of the first motorbikes was built in 1885 in Germany. It had a wooden frame and wooden wheels. Today's motorbikes are made mostly of metal and plastic.

This motorbike is called the
Silent Grey Fellow.

Around 1900, companies began making motorbikes for
people to buy. One of these motorbike companies was
Harley-Davidson. Harley-Davidson became one of the
most popular makers of motorbikes.

Classic Motorbikes

Classic motorbikes look good as well as feel good to ride.

A classic motorbike is an old motorbike that is famous because of the way it looks. The Harley-Davidson 45 is a classic motorbike. It was made in the 1940s.

Collectors keep their classic motorbikes shiny and in perfect condition.

Many people enjoy collecting classic motorbikes. They spend hours repairing, cleaning, and polishing them. Collectors often display their bikes at classic motorbike shows.

Where Motorbikes Are Used

Most motorbikes are used on roads that have a smooth surface. Riding a motorbike is a good way of getting around quickly. Many people use them in busy towns and cities.

In countries where there are many people, motorbikes are useful for driving to work and school.

Motorbikes do not take up much space on a narrow road.

In some places, roads are very narrow. It is hard for cars to drive along these roads. Motorbikes are a good way to get around these places.

Mopeds

A moped is like a bicycle with a small **engine** attached. Mopeds are cheap to buy and easy to use. Riders often use a moped when they are first learning to ride a motorbike.

Mopeds are smaller than other motorbikes.

pedal

The pedals on a moped
help it to keep up speed.

A moped has pedals like the pedals on a bicycle.
The rider pedals to start the engine. The pedals
also give extra power when going up steep hills.

Scooters

A scooter has much smaller wheels than a normal motorbike. Many people ride scooters to get to work. In some countries, teenagers ride them for fun.

Scooters can be small, but they can still carry two people.

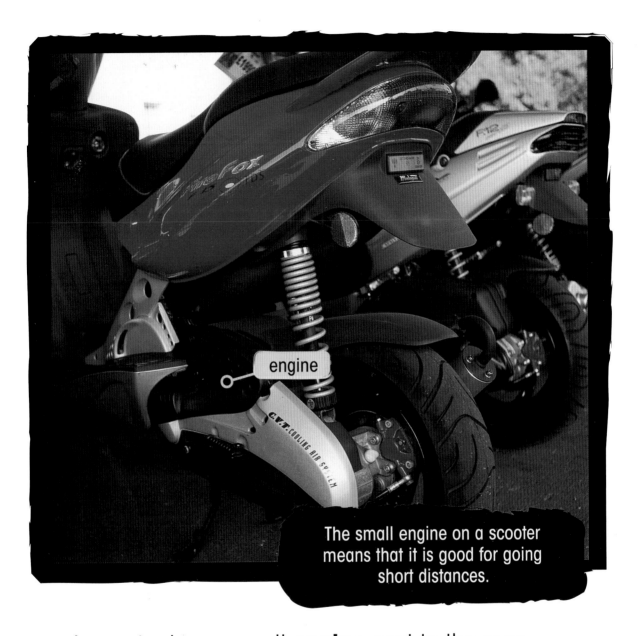

engine

The small engine on a scooter means that it is good for going short distances.

A scooter has a small **engine** next to the rear wheel. The engine moves the scooter by making the rear wheel turn. The rider's seat is above the engine.

Superbikes

Riders can race against each other on very powerful motorbikes called superbikes. These bikes can ride along at nearly 185 miles (300 kilometers) per hour.

Superbikes have large engines and can go very fast.

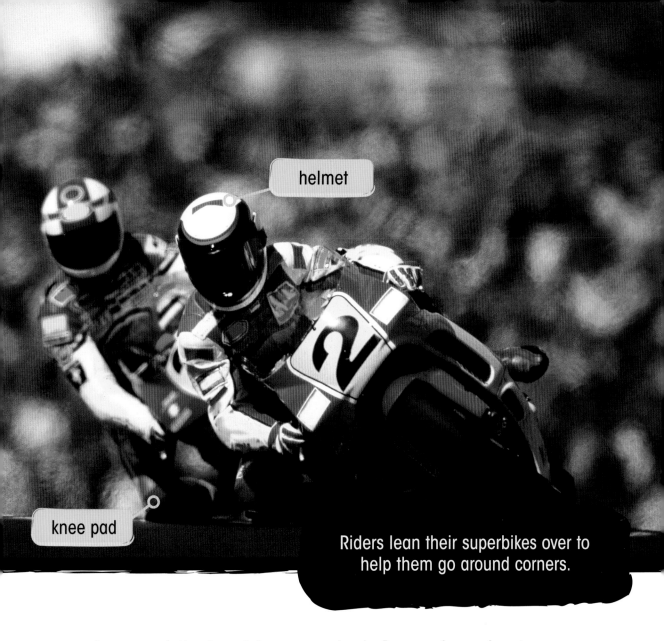

helmet

knee pad

Riders lean their superbikes over to help them go around corners.

A superbike's wide, rounded **tires** give plenty of grip to stop it from skidding. The riders wear special clothing, such as pads to protect their knees.

Motocross Bikes

A motocross bike is used for racing over hilly, bumpy **dirt tracks**. The riders often slide their feet along the ground. This helps them to keep from falling over.

Motocross racing on dirt tracks is a popular sport in some countries.

Motocross bikes have **tires** with a chunky **tread** that grips the muddy ground well. The wheels have strong, springy **suspension** for going over bumps and jumps.

suspension

Riders get very dirty while racing and jumping their motocross bikes.

Touring Motorbikes

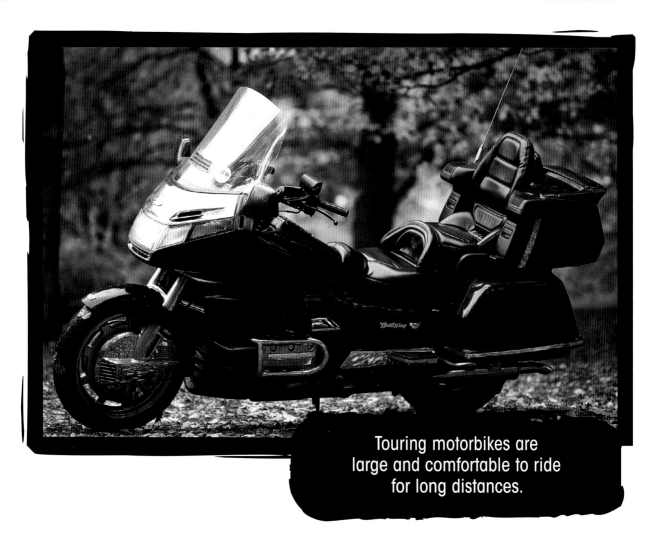

Touring motorbikes are large and comfortable to ride for long distances.

Touring motorbikes are for riders who want to go on long journeys. They are big motorbikes. They have **engines** that are as big and powerful as car engines.

Saddlebags can hold clothes and other items so the rider can go on a trip on the motorbike.

saddlebag

At the back of a touring motorbike is a luggage rack. On the rack there are luggage containers called saddlebags. There is also an extra seat called a pillion for a passenger.

Patrol Bikes

Police officers use patrol bikes to get quickly to the scenes of accidents or crimes. The bikes they use are special touring motorbikes. The motorbikes are fitted with **two-way radios**.

Police motorbikes are large and fast.

Police patrol bikes have flashing lights and loud **sirens**. The lights and sirens warn drivers and **pedestrians** that the bike is coming. This gives people a chance to move out of the way.

Police motorbikes have some of the same equipment as police patrol cars do, such as radios and flashing lights.

Sidecars

Some motorbikes have sidecars. A sidecar has a seat for a passenger inside. Together, the motorbike and the sidecar are called a combination motorbike.

sidecar

Sidecars allow a driver to bring a passenger along.

A sidecar has its own wheel. This means that a combination motorbike has three wheels. The motorbike rider on a combination motorbike cannot lean it over to go around corners.

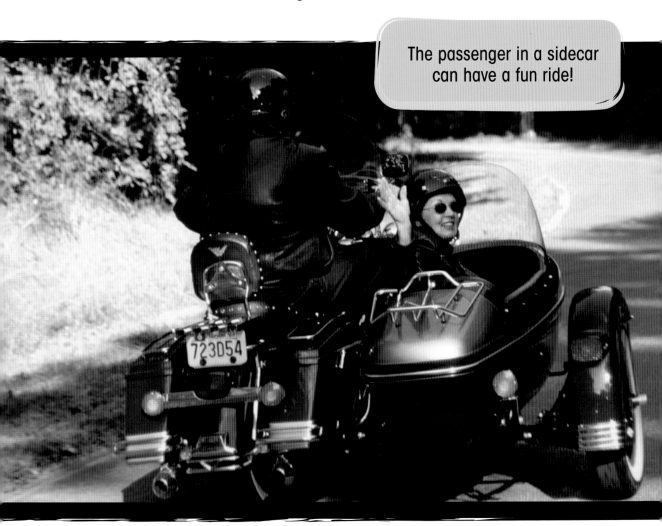

The passenger in a sidecar can have a fun ride!

Motorbike Taxis

In some countries, the streets buzz with three-wheeled motorbikes. They are called rickshaws. Many rickshaws are used as taxis.

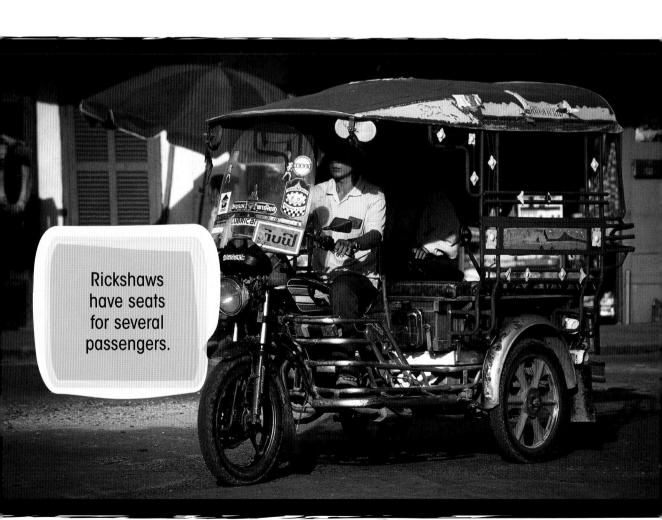

Rickshaws have seats for several passengers.

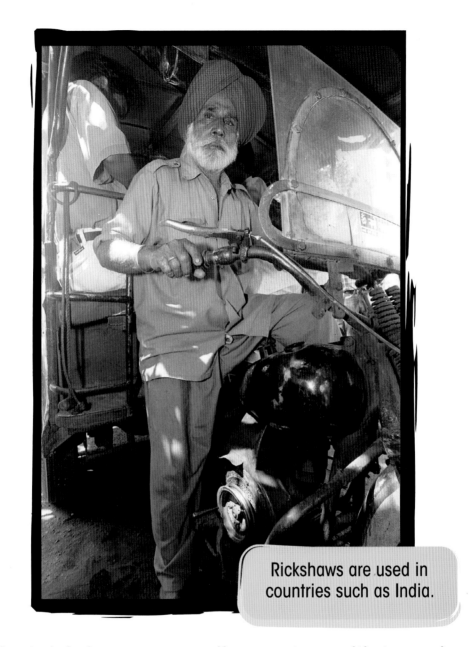

Rickshaws are used in countries such as India.

Most rickshaws are really scooters with two wheels at the back instead of one. They can be easier to drive in crowded areas than a normal taxi. The driver sits at the front and steers using handlebars.

Timeline

1868   Two brothers named Pierre and Ernest Michaux fit a steam **engine** to a bicycle to make a simple motorbike.

1885   Two German engineers named Gottlieb Daimler and Wilhelm Maybach build one of the first motorbikes. It has a small gasoline engine.

1907   The first TT motorbike races are held. The races are still held today. TT stands for Tourist Trophy.

1950s   The first scooters are built in Italy. They become popular for teenagers to ride in the 1960s.

1968   The world's first superbike is shown at the Tokyo Motor Show. It is the Honda CB750.

2006   Denis Manning of the United States breaks the world record for speed on a specially built motorbike. He travels at 350 miles (564 kilometers) per hour.

Glossary

dirt tracks   narrow dirt road

engine   machine that powers movement using fuel

fuel   substance that burns to make heat. Motorbikes use gasoline as fuel for their engines.

pedestrian   person traveling by foot

rubber   soft, flexible material used to make tires for vehicles

siren   device that makes a loud warning noise

suspension   system of springs that lets a motorbike's wheels move up and down over bumps

tire   rubber ring that fits around the outside of a wheel. It has a chunky tread on the outside and is filled with air.

tread   pattern of grooves around the outside of a tire. The tread makes the tires grip on wet or muddy roads.

two-way radio   radio that lets you talk and listen to someone else

Find Out More

Graham, Ian. *Motorbikes.* Chicago: Raintree, 2006.

Hill, Lee Sullivan. *Motorcycles.* Minneapolis, MN: Lerner, 2004.

Tiner, John Hudson. *Motorcycles.* Mankato, MN: Creative
    Education, 2004.

Index